This book belo

This book is dedicated to my children – Mikey, Kobe, and Jojo.

Paperback ISBN: 978-1-63731-565-1
Hardcover ISBN: 978-1-63731-567-5
eBook ISBN: 978-1-63731-566-8

Printed and bound in the USA.
NinjaLifeHacks.tv

Ninja Life Hacks™

NINJAS
Go to Space

Ninja Life Hacks

By Mary Nhin

Late at night when the stars are out,
Motivated Ninja dares to dream
Of travelling through space,
To brand new worlds and galactic scenes.

And then, it was finally time,
Everything was in place.
5 ... 4 ... 3 ... 2 ... 1 ... BLAST OFF!
Ninja was going to space!

They didn't visit Uranus,
But went to Neptune, for sure.
And after running around Saturn's rings,
They felt dizzier than before!

When they landed on Mars,
They couldn't believe their eyes.
Aliens were running around **EVERYWHERE**!
What an amazing surprise.

And as Ninja flew back towards Earth,
Taking in the beautiful view,
Ninja thought, *When you dream big and work hard,
There's nothing that you can't do!*

I love to hear from my readers. Write to me at growgritpress@gmail.com and let me know your ideas for my next book!

Yours truly, Mary Nhin

 @marynhin @GrowGrit #NinjaLifeHacks

 Ninja Life Hacks

 Mary Nhin Ninja Life Hacks

 @ninjalifehacks.tv

Made in the USA
Middletown, DE
10 November 2022